Memoir
of
Neuengamme
Concentration Camp

MEMOIR OF NEUENGAMME CONCENTRATION CAMP

By Pieter Laning
Translated from Dutch by Dineke Laning
Edited by Peter van der Schoor

Published by Klaas Laning
Hobart, Tasmania

Copyright © 2022 by Klaas Laning

All rights reserved. Except as permitted under the Australian Copyright Act 1968 (for example, a fair dealing for the purposes of study, research, criticism or review), no part of this book may be reproduced, stored in a retrieval system, communicated or transmitted in any form or by any means without prior written permission. All inquiries should be made to the publisher.

First edition published in English in 2023 by Klaas Laning in Australia.

First published in Dutch on 1 August 1980 by Pieter Laning and Gerard Boekhoven.

First translated by Dineke Laning in 1980, with later additions and amendments by Peter van der Schoor and Klaas Laning.

Klaas Laning
15 Osborne Esplanade
Kingston Beach, Tasmania 7050

National Library of Australia Cataloguing In-Publication Data:
    Laning, Pieter
    Memoir of Neuengamme Concentration Camp

Cover design by Melita Eagling

Paperback

Memoir of Neuengamme Concentration Camp/Pieter Laning -- 1st ed.

ISBN 978-0-646-87690-0

1. Memoir 2. World War Two 3. Concentration Camp, Neuengamme 4. The Bay of Lübeck 5. Cap Arcona

Dedication

This book is dedicated to our father, Pieter Laning, who endured so much pain and suffering whilst incarcerated and yet took the time to write down his memories, and to our mother, Dineke Laning, who translated those memories into English whilst it was not her native tongue. They both live large in our memories.

Contents

Introduction 1
Chapter I 2
    16 January 1945 2
    16 March 2
    17 March 2
    19 March 3
Chapter II 3
Chapter III 5
Chapter IV 6
    20 March 7
Chapter V 7
Chapter VI 8
Chapter VII 10
Chapter VIII 11
Chapter IX 12
Chapter X 13
    26 March 14
Chapter XI 15
    28 March 16
Chapter XII 16
Chapter XIII 18
Chapter XIV 19
Chapter XV 20
Chapter XVI 22
Chapter XVII 23
Chapter XVIII 24

Chapter XIX	25
Chapter XX	27
Chapter XXI	28
Chapter XXII	29
Chapter XXIII	30
Chapter XXIV	31
Chapter XXV	32
Chapter XXVI	33
Chapter XXVII	34
Chapter XXVIII	35
Chapter XXIX	36
Chapter XXX	37
Chapter XXXI	38
Chapter XXXII	39
Chapter XXXIII	40
Chapter XXXIV	42
Chapter XXXV	43
Chapter XXXVI	45
Chapter XXXVII	46
Chapter XXXVIII	47
Chapter XXXIX	48
Chapter XL	49
Chapter XLI	50
Chapter XLII	51
Chapter XLIII	52
Glossary	57
Acknowledgements	59
The author and the translator	61

Table of Figures

Figure 1: Aerial photo of Neuengamme Concentration Camp from *Nederlanders in Neuengamme* by Dr Judith Schuyf. xiii

Figure 2: Map of concentration camps under NS rule during World War Two with Neuengamme Concentration Camp circled from *Nederlanders in Neuengamme* by Dr Judith Schuyf. xv

Figure 3: Excerpt from the handwritten memoir of Pieter Laning, Chapter XV. 21

Figure 4: Excerpt from the handwritten memoir of Pieter Laning, Chapter XIX. 26

Figure 5: Excerpt from the handwritten memoir of Pieter Laning, Chapter XXXIII 41

Figure 6: Pieter and Dineke Laning, 1976 61

Figure 1: Aerial photo of Neuengamme Concentration Camp from *Nederlanders in Neuengamme* by Dr Judith Schuyf.

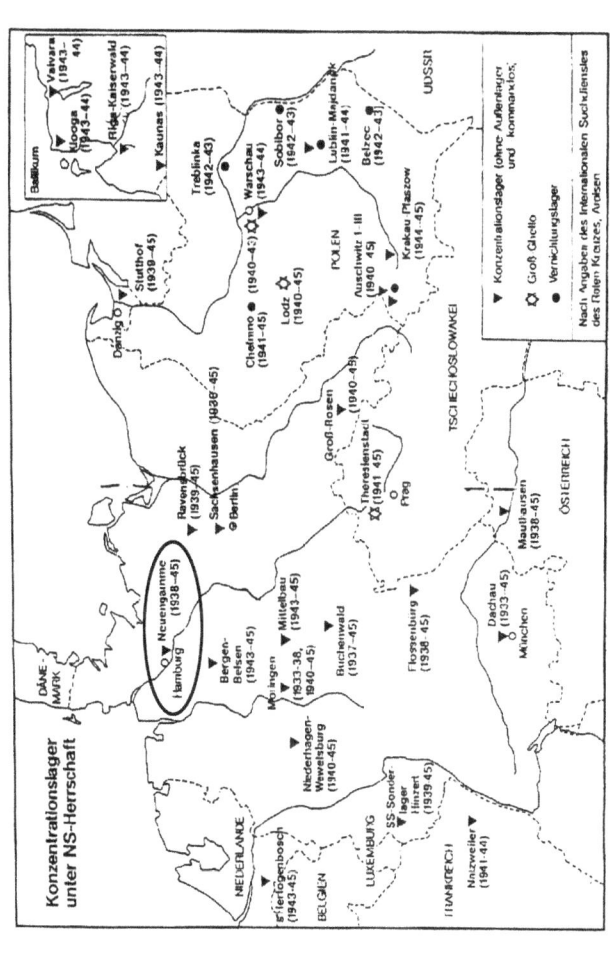

Belangrijkste concentratiekampen.

Figure 2: Map of concentration camps under NS rule during World War Two with Neuengamme Concentration Camp circled from *Nederlanders in Neuengamme* by Dr Judith Schuyf.

Introduction

The *Memoir of Neuengamme* commences with an account of what happened on 16 January 1945 in cell 33 in the *Huis van Bewaring* (prison) in Groningen. To get a better understanding of what went on, I think it fitting to remember a few things concerning the events preceding the situation.

We start with September 1944, the month in which the unsuccessful allied air force landing in Arnhem took place. Our hope for a quick liberation was dashed. The activities of the S.D. and SS increased and daily there were arrests and executions. The prisons were crowded, so too the Huis van Bewaring. It was more crowded than ever before. Quite often there were six or seven people in a one-person cell.

In cell 33 there were four people: Jan Pot from Veendam, Heino Bult, Henk Rolsma and me. Heino, Jan and I were arrested in connection with the resistance group called "Roelof" (Heidema), who with nearly all his fellow workers was also imprisoned. What happened to this group has been recorded in this memoir.

Even now, after 35 years, all are in our thoughts. The terrible things that happened have stayed with us all along. Not a day passes without us thinking of those who have not been blessed in the same way as we who were able to return.

Chapter I

16 January 1945

Today is Heino's wedding anniversary. Three years ago, he was married. He tells us over and over how good his wife is, and we gladly believe him. At 3 am it is very noisy. We know that this means transport. We too? Our door opens and Jan and Heino are called. We are all petrified and very nervous. Does this mean a farewell forever? When it is time, I embrace each of them and find it very hard. I wonder why I am not called. I belong to them! However, our cell stays closed and we remain, just the two of us, Henk and I.

16 March

At 4 am we are woken and when we go down the stairs we find out that a large group is being transported. With a lot of noise and screaming, we are put in the downstairs cells. We have to wait for the following transportation. After several months I see my friends again and make new ones as well.

17 March

In the evening we leave in cars and go to the railway station where in groups of 50 people we are put into an animal carriage guarded by Dutch *Grune Polizei*. After a waiting period of some hours, we depart (Sunday morning 18 March 4 am) and it proves to be a large transportation. Prisoners from Amersfoort and Assen are also with us. We are in good spirits. I had received a large suitcase from my family and they had included some tobacco so we were all smoking. Harry Diemer, a biologist, is next to me. There are also three ministers, one from Warnsveld, his name is Rienk Kuiper and he has nine children. When we pass the border, we have an unpleasant feeling as we face uncertainty for the future. May the Lord be our helper and shield.

19 March

We have been in the carriage for three days now, almost without any sleep. We have to wait as the railway tracks are damaged. We see Hamburg or rather the ruins of the city. Terrible damage or rather devastation. Tommies (British pilots) fly over our heads time and again and we hear bombs coming down. At such times we stay locked up and the guards look for a safe place. When the doors are closed, we pray together. Rienk leads us in prayer. Late at night we arrive at the camp. It's 12 midnight and one carriage after another is emptied, while lots of floodlights are shining and we are heavily guarded.

Chapter II

The first beatings are given out and hard ones at that. I have a heavy suitcase and have difficulty in keeping up with the others. I got a beating with a rifle butt, which makes me go faster. Well, that's the beginning and with God's grace we will make it. As we walk the lights shine on us. We see many high buildings surrounded by high fences made of barbed wire, which are electrified. At last, we come to the entrance of what we come to know as the concentration camp. It is very depressing also as machine guns are constantly aimed at us. We come to a large building and have to go into the cellar. This goes together with beatings from the so-called *Kapos*, who are in charge. They are criminals and murderers and are recognised by a band around their sleeves with the word Kapo on it. On the left they have a triangle and a number. The triangles have different colours, red stands for political prisoner, green for a murderer or burglar and black indicates the prisoner is a homosexual. These are all men who have been in camp for more than 10 years and who have little humanity left in them. They always carry a policeman's baton with them and make plenty of use of it. We then come into a large cellar where several hundred people can fit. It smells stuffy and we can see that people work here daily. There are large benches and small tables, and on the floor large heaps of scraps of tyres. We are pushed to the other end. Tired and exhausted we long for some rest and food. Mr Zuidhof, who on transport already showed symptoms of insanity, is getting worse. At long last our names are called and in groups of 50 we go upstairs, again accompanied by beatings with the batons. They hurt terribly and to escape these I start looking beforehand where these men are standing. In the dark we trudge towards a large building where we learn that we have to be washed, deloused and shaven all over. This is the first big shame we have to endure.

Chapter III

We are all beaten and pushed into a large hall where we have to undress completely. The only things we are allowed to keep are our shoes, toiletries and tobacco. Our rings, watches, etc., if we still possess them, are taken from us. In return we receive a metal plate with a number on it together with a string so we can hang it around our necks. There is a lot of noise and bashing and during the commotion a Kapo sees fit to take my packet of tobacco, nothing I can do about it. I get a kick on my behind and land in the *Waschraum*. What I see and experience here I will never forget.

It is a large room with eight wooden tables on one side. In front of every table stands a Kapo with a razor. On the other side are showers or douches. We are all standing in a row naked, and kneel in turn in front of the first Kapo, who shaves our head. This goes very fast. The next Kapo lathers the other parts of our bodies that have to be shaven and we have to lie on a table for the following Kapo to handle that. Before it's my turn I see Harry Diemer and Rienk Kuiper go through the ordeal. I observe that Harry and Rienk choose not to be humiliated by this treatment. Then it's my turn. As bald as a coot we stand under the shower. Each treatment takes only two or three minutes. After this we come into a dressing room where they hand out (Kapo-style) parcels of underwear which we put on over wet bodies. They are old and far too big and in the meantime we are beaten to make us hurry up. An old minister from Apeldoorn is beaten mercilessly by a Polish Kapo with a nasty look on his face. Then we receive our other outfit which is not much more than rags. Before we have a chance to put them on, we are already outside. It's cold and dark and everything goes so fast that we scarcely realise what has happened. It is appalling and for the first time I feel very disheartened.

Chapter IV

Most people have lost all the things they were allowed to take. I have managed to save some tobacco and my soap but the rest I lost too. My suitcase with all that was in it, my clothes and my backpack. But we have no time to think about it, as we have to go again. We arrive at barracks where we get one bunk bed per two persons. I share mine with Harry D and as we lie down, we cannot sleep and keep talking about our first impressions. Everything has gone so quickly and we are so confounded that we just keep on talking. The barrack is overcrowded. Beds three high and each with two people in it. The rags we took off we use as cover as it is very cold. The rags are horrible and make us look like tramps and all the more because our heads are bald. The rags are too big or too small with a strip of different kinds of material. This different strip means we will be easily recognised in the event of escape. All these things we discuss over and over again, and we are sure that we will not have a good time here. Towards three o'clock we fall asleep.

20 March

With great racket and the shout "*Aufstehen*" we are woken up. We did not sleep much and it was short. Outside it is still dark so it must be early. Someone calls, "*Schnell, schnell!*" and hundreds of men start moving. The first beatings begin again. Well, we will get used to that. When we are dressed, we know how terrible we look in our clothing. Ah well, we have to take that too. Outside we have *Appell* (roll call) and have to stand in rows of five. After having been counted about 10 times, we are allowed to go back into the barracks where we get our "breakfast", which also has to go in fast tempo. We have to eat standing up, as there is no room for everyone to sit. We receive a thin slice of bread each and a bowl of coffee to share between two men. Now it will start.

Chapter V

The following days are full of impressions we will never forget. The camp consists of tens of large stone buildings, in between are about 15 wooden barracks, which are each surrounded by barbed wire. In the middle is a large square, where we have to go on roll call each morning, afternoon and night. We are there with thousands of men from all countries and everyone looks atrocious. They all look skinny and with a hunted look on their face. We have to get used to that, knowing it will also be our future. We pass the so-called "*Revier*" (sick bay) and hundreds of *kranken* (sick people). They hang out of the windows and ask for cigarettes. These people are not humans anymore, they are skeletons, living corpses. They lie with three people to a single bunk bed and the majority are suffering with dysentery — an illness that is feared by all as it saps your strength. I have never seen more misery and it frightens us. Every morning 80 or 90 dead people are thrown out onto a wagon, their last journey to the "crematorium", which is in operation day and night. I have seen many wagons go that way, loaded with corpses, but the horse could easily pull the wagon as the corpses did not weigh more than about 40 kilograms. The crematorium is next to the kitchen and the one takes care that the other has enough to do.

From other people we hear that the camp is nowadays a health resort compared to what it has been in the past. Last winter people were beaten to death. Still every day about 80 to 90 people die. The largest number so far was in the month of February, when the number rose to 2,000. The day the doctor told us this 123 people died.

In January, 5,000 men went on transport to Husum. By the end of the month, 1,000 returned, 800 of these were *muzelmannen* (walking skeletons). Truly, a great success for the SS! We see some men from the SS with murderous faces. When they pass us, we stand to attention with cap in hand. It's all prescribed!

Chapter VI

The men from the SS all carry a whip and whip anyone, who comes close to them, in the face. I saw two people who were thus beaten up while they were standing to attention. Just for their pleasure! Gerard Boekhoven knows about it. I had a little bit of tobacco left, but that was stolen from me during roll call. Cigarettes are exchanged for a full ration of bread. People prefer to smoke rather than eat. Standing at roll call is certainly no fun. Sometimes more than an hour. Compared to some months ago it's nothing. At that time, they had roll call in the middle of the night. Sometimes three to four hours standing in knee-deep snow and icy cold weather. In twos and threes, they fell down and nobody was allowed to help them stand up again. Several men died on such nights. They were picked up from where they had dropped dead, the next morning, and brought to the crematorium with others who had died in the Revier (sick bay)! The crematorium is always hungry!

On the same day we received some very bad news. All except one of our large group of Roelof, which left on 16 January, is dead. This is terrible news and we are crushed. Ten of them died in the Revier and 49 were hanged. It's terrible and we cannot get it out of our minds. I think of Jan and Heino and of all the friends I knew so well and with whom I worked. All dead! It was passed on to us by Camphuis, the only one left from the group. We also hear that Wil Niemeyer had perished during bombing of Hamburg. The hanging of the 49 happened in daytime on 20 and 21 February in a bunker. All were from Holland. Ten of them had been in the Revier and were very sick at the time of the hanging. There was no mercy. One can't fathom the mentality of the SS. They must have an alliance with the devil.

Chapter VII

Camp life is not easy and we soon lose weight. It also shows on our faces. Not so much because of the shortage of food but more so due to lack of sleep and the constant tension we endure. Also, the times of air raid alarm are unbearable, especially at night. Then we are bullied and beaten out of the barracks and have scarcely time to put on even trousers and shoes. We are pushed into a cellar with hundreds at a time, pushed together with Poles, Russians and other nationalities. And the terrible smell that hangs in that stuffy area! In the daytime hundreds of sick people work here braiding rubber mats. I have seen how they were tortured by Kapos. Poor fellows! Two of them were doctors from Holland. Their eyes were inflamed and their hands full of sores, which were infected. One coughing, miserable crowd ready for the crematorium. During the nights their smell stays in the cellar, never to be aired. Truly a sad company of overtired people. After a few hours we are allowed to go back to the barrack, trying to get some more sleep. Sometimes when we come back, we discover that the few things we still possessed have vanished, blanket included. The Russians mostly take these. Here they call it, "organising". Those who can do that live the longest. The Russians all look rather healthy.

Some days later we get numbers sewn onto our jackets and trousers. That also goes in fast tempo combined with beatings. Zuidhof is now completely out of his mind and walks around with a big patch on his coat. On this patch is the number of the barrack to which he belongs. He walks around without knowing what he is doing. It's a sad sight.

Also in these days, 64 men are taken out of the group. They receive a tag with the word "*Torsperre*" on it and have to put it on their right arm. These are people who are known to have a death penalty and have to wait for the execution order, which has to come from Berlin. Gerard Boekhoven is one of them.

Chapter VIII

The people with the word "Torsperre" on their arm are not allowed out of the camp, not even under supervision. They are the severe cases and are separated from us. They receive different treatment and are placed in barrack 10, which is even more reinforced with barbed wire. It does not look very good.

Roelof and his group went through the same trauma. It's a day for great sorrow when they leave us. Still, we are pleased that we don't belong to them. They will be executed sooner or later. We still have a chance of going back home. This is how we reason in a very selfish manner. Can you expect anything else in such circumstances?

However, camp life goes on. Little to eat and much beating, if you are not careful. You cannot always escape it, and one gets more than the other. It goes the same way with the meals. The Russians usually get the most. Each day half a litre of soup, which consists of water with swedes, not even a potato in it. It's like dishwater! In the morning and at teatime we receive one slice of bread with a little bit of margarine and occasionally a small piece of sausage. No wonder we are hungry and when you are really hungry you talk about food all day. What you did not like in earlier days, you would love to have now. However, there is not much time to dwell on it because during the work hours you have to be on the lookout for the Kapos or the SS.

Personally, I think very little about home as everything is so new and the tension is enormous. Our work consists of digging. It's not too heavy but the lack of food and the unusual job cause us to be exhausted at night-time. When you come back to the barracks and receive your rations, you consume it as quickly as possible out of fear of the Russians, who will take it from you if they have a chance. They help one another in this and make use of the crowded area.

Chapter IX

The area we live in has three rows of bunk beds, three high. We are there with hundreds of men. No privacy! We also have among us a doctor from Holland as prisoner. He is an old hand by now. He gives us several valuable tips or hints. His name is Dr Vlim and he lives in Leiden. He especially warns us not to drink water here as it has a high chlorine content and is bad for the intestines. He is quite right as there are quite a few in our group who drank much water and have already developed dysentery. Also, the morale is going down. The beatings, the stress and long roll calls are just too much for many. One sees it on their faces.

These people try to hang on to you and complain about being tired. They lose their willpower and continue to drink water as much as possible. But the sight of patients in the Revier and the warnings of the doctor help us to refrain from drinking water. According to the doctor the SS prefers us to die from ordinary illnesses. Some men from our group also start showing symptoms of giving up. The road to the crematorium is very short! As regards spiritual food, that is also scarce and is actually forbidden. No Bibles are allowed in the camp. Members of the SS are like beasts and are working together with the devil. Every morning we see wagons full of corpses. Yes, the trenches around Groningen are paid for dearly! As are all the men who fought for freedom.

Chapter X

But no matter how miserable it may be here, with regard to the war, it goes well and will probably not last much longer. With the help of the Lord, we may be able to get out of this place. Spirits are good and we encourage each other as much as possible. Most of the time I am with Harry Diemer and Rienk Kuiper. We always look for one another and find strength from each other. Rienk preaches a short sermon between the barracks and closes in communal prayer. We were all moved by it and could not hide our tears. It has been our last Sunday together.

26 March

The following day there is a large transportation of 500 men. I am included, while Harry and Rienk stay behind. I have no time to say farewell and am absorbed into the big crowd. Fortunately, I see several friends, which makes me feel rather safe and happy in the circumstances we are in. Destination is unknown. Accompanied by the SS and the big German shepherd dogs, we go to the train that is on the campsite. We go, 70 men to a carriage plus eight guards for whom we have to leave quite a bit of room, for their comfort. There is no straw, neither do we have blankets. We just have to wait and see. The first day has passed and we are still locked up in the carriage on the campsite while night is approaching. We have nothing to eat or to drink and we feel very miserable. We ask one of the guards for food, but he laughs at us. We have to face the night just like that. Sleeping is impossible as we have scarcely room to sit. It has been a terrible night. It has lasted so long and we are all hungry. Spirits are low and we are getting crabby with each other. Some suffer from dysentery. They have to use the *Kiebel*, which is a drum without lid, serving as our toilet. The stench is atrocious, all those people, and just one stinking drum. The situation is unbearable. The morning also passes by without food, which makes it a day and a half without anything. In the afternoon we each receive a bowl of water, which tastes delicious as we are parched.

Chapter XI

The day passes again without food. In the evening we receive a quarter of a litre of soup, but not everyone gets it, as there is not enough. The atmosphere is one of great dissatisfaction, besides there are some very sick people, which certainly does not improve people's moods. We all see sickness as our future. Will we be able to endure? We do hope so. By nine o'clock in the evening we start moving. At long last! Wherever we might be going, we at least are on the way, even if the night means horror. In the middle of the night, we arrive in Hamburg and remain in the carriage till the morning. We receive our first ration of bread since leaving the barracks and it tastes delicious, regardless of the foul smell that is getting worse all the time. The sick are going downhill very fast, their eyes are becoming enlarged, and they are most likely not going to make it much longer. From time to time the doors will be opened for a moment and we see Hamburg, at least what it once was. We see no more than heaps of ruins as far as we are able to look. We look right through the city. Good on you, Tommies! Everything has to go! But they also visit us and those are anxious moments. The bombs come down like rain and the noise is frightening, yet we are calm, we know we are in God's hands.

After this event the train starts moving again. How long! We are sitting on sores and everything aches. We don't know what to do with ourselves and we are also terribly thirsty. In these two days we have only had some soup and a slice of bread and feel miserable due to hunger. Oh, how I think of home and of the food I did not like! Now it would mean a banquet! The trip takes long, and we are all worn out. In the corner lies the first dead man, but we do not seem to care about it. Soon a second one will follow. We only think about ourselves. Yes, that is the way it goes with mankind under such circumstances. One is only interested in his best friend in such a situation and that is again out of selfishness. At long last we stop, having arrived at our destination. We drag ourselves out of the carriage and, for the first time since our departure, breathe in some fresh air.

28 March

It is 28 March, and we are pleased that we are now at the destination. It's the small city of Melzen and it is nicely situated on Lüneburger Heide heathland. But we are not interested in what is nice, we are hungry and thirsty and go as quickly as possible to our "retreat".

Chapter XII

This is an old shed belonging to a sugar factory and the two attics have been made ready for us. When we arrive there, we immediately fall down onto the straw, as we also had to stand for an hour and a half on roll call in front of the factory. We are pleased to be able to lie down. We don't get any food, but at least we are allowed to sleep, though we don't know what is more important at this stage: food or sleep. But we still know we won't get any food anyway, so we settle down for the night. Those who have "special friendship" with someone soon find each other. There are no bunk beds, we are all lying next to one another in the straw. The SS has a special purpose. If they can't break you physically, they will try to do it mentally and they have seen to that very well. The moral standards have become very low. The Kapos also have their "friends" next to them when they sleep. The youngest one is a 17-year-old Polish boy. These are spoiled by the Kapos and receive more food and some cigarettes. The whole night we sleep well and consequently we are in a better mood. Now something to eat! And indeed, we are getting some bread. Washing ourselves is scarcely possible as there are 500 men on two attics and there are only 10 taps, actually a long horizontal pipe with 10 holes giving not much more than a trickle of water, the size of a knitting needle. At least the "camp" spirit is not so strong here, though beatings are still a normal thing. After breakfast there is a roll call again. As long as there is no work for us yet, there is sure to be a roll call more often. And true it is, one after another. After two days we leave the square at half past six and go to the railway station. There we see a whole lot of rubble that was caused six weeks ago. Well done, Tommies! Good shot! We count 12 locomotive engines completely ruined. Furthermore, a long row of carriages all badly damaged. From the station itself nothing is to be seen anymore. Hundreds of carriages are irreparable. Totally destroyed. Even about 10 heavy "Jumbos" all gone to pieces.

Chapter XIII

All railway tracks are out of place, some stick high up into the air. We enjoy the sight of it, but do not dare to show it. You just have to keep straight faces. We have to go right through the rubble and end up at the very end of the railway tracks, where the garden allotment is. The road runs along it and has large craters and thrown-about parts of railway carriages. Here we have to work. The craters have to be filled in and the leftover parts of the carriages have to be removed. This is a heavy and unusual job. After we have worked for an hour, we are all exhausted. The people with dysentery want to rest for a moment, but the beatings bring them back to work again. These poor people just can't hold it in and have to let it run out of their trousers. It's just blood and water. They can never live long. It is just slavery, for the beatings are severe. I am getting my share too and the anger of the Kapo just falls onto my back, which means a sleepless night. Ah well, we go on and hopefully come out of this mess. Three men fall down and can't go on anymore. When the SS arrives, there is a lot of beating with the cudgels on our backs, for if the Kapo does not do it to us, the SS will do it to the Kapo. That is their whole system. The SS have a look at the three sick men and kick them in the stomach. They writhe in pain, but cannot get up. After that they are left alone. And now the Kapo is being told off. The work is not good enough and we are not positioned in the right way. When the SS have left, we have a repeat of what happened earlier and receive beatings on our backs again. We get nothing to eat and work through till half past five, which means 10 hours and we are broken. We just drag ourselves over the uneven plot and hand in our spades and mattocks. Then there is roll call and at last we move on.

Chapter XIV

We pass long rows of English war prisoners who work on the same plot of land. They look well and are getting better treatment, too. They also receive parcels from the Red Cross. Compared to them we look like tramps. Our clothes are already torn, and we look pale and worn out, and we have no energy. When we walk, we drag ourselves through the city. On the way we receive more beatings. I get one under my chin and a kick in the behind. A small Kapo does it. He looks Jewish and wears a black triangle (H.S.) I must have annoyed him by the way I looked for I receive another punch. Well, that's enough for me. We come back and have to stand on roll call straight away. It's seven o'clock in the meantime and we're still standing outside. The three sick people came with us with the help of some friends but are now lying on the ground again, unconscious.

Chapter XV

We never find meat in our soup. It's always soup, sago and soup again. And if you are the first one to receive a bowlful from a full pot, you get nothing but water and eight or nine cubes of swede. The person who is last may find a few pieces of potato. That is a real treat, but also an exception. When we finish eating, we take off some of our clothes and lie on them or put them under our heads, as otherwise they would be gone. Those who still have some shaving things bind them to their bodies, otherwise the Russians will take them and offer them to you the next day in return for some cigarettes. It's no use to tell the Kapo, for he will just beat you up. You have to eat your bread straight away, otherwise that will go too. Anyway, it's really not possible to keep some bread for later. That only happens to the ones that suffer from dysentery. They only drink water and this water has the same problem as that in Neuengamme. It only makes your condition worse. By now we have another sensation, we have lice! Real lice, black, white and red. I had already slept restlessly for some nights and then we discovered what the cause was. The first time I catch 22, but soon after I cannot count them anymore. Our singlets are black with them. We are red all over and, twice a day, we have "catching sessions". We pick them from everywhere, which is an unsightly business. We sit there naked doing this ghastly business every night; they seem to like the crotch best of all. After that we go to sleep. Life here exists of beatings, work, sleep and lastly taking a bit of food.

de jongens die dat presteren
zijn in de spuit paap, want dat
wordt steeds erger. Ze drinken
zich dik en het water is van het-
zelfde gehalte als in Neurenca-
mie." En hier moet je maar
op jezelf passen.

Afgaans krijgen we er een
nieuwe genosch bij, want wij
hebben luizen, eerste luizen.
Fooie, witte en helemaal zwar-
ten. Ik heb al een paar keer erg
onrustig geslapen en al gauw
kwamen we tot de ontdekking
dat het luizen waren. De eerste
keer ving ik er 22 maar enige
dagen daarna konden we ze niet
meer tellen. Het zag zwart in
ons hemd. Ons lichaam zit
vol rooie stippen en nu zijn we
gewoon verplicht om tenminste
per dag twee maal te luizen."
's avonds zit ieder dat onmake-
lijke werk te verrichten. We zitten
hen om nakie en halen ze van ons
lichaam. Vooral in het kruis zitten erg veel. Dan is ons hemd aan
de beurt en als dat "schoon" is
gaan we slapen. Zoo is het
leven hier, slaag, luiken en
slapen, eten komt op de vierde
plaats.

Figure 3: Excerpt from the handwritten memoir of Pieter Laning, Chapter XV.

Chapter XVI

During the past fortnight, we did not work much. There were often air-raid alarms, and it seems as if the frontier is closer by. At the sound of the alarm, we run over the field to a safer place. It gives us a chance to pick up a swede or onion growing in the field. While we lie in a ditch for cover, we enjoy eating whatever we can get hold of in such a situation. Sometimes we find only peels of the swedes, but we eat them just as well. These are our best moments. Lying on our backs, chewing as long as possible and seeing and hearing hundreds of Tommies go over.

One day a group of planes parted from the formation and came right down over Uelzen. How scared we were at that time! A deafening noise, screeching machines and the whistle of bombs coming towards us. It was frightening! It all came in a few seconds. When we go through the city, we see the havoc. Ruins still smoking, while people frantically look for men, women and children who may be buried under the rubble. We see many corpses, terribly mutilated. They are all put on a heap. Whole bodies as well as parts of them. It is awful to look at. What devastation even a few bombs can cause! Whole streets that were intact in the morning now lie in ruins. Trees are lying over the streets and water spurts out of pipes. We struggle through all this to the factory. For the first time I cannot eat. From the factory we can look on to the road and see long rows of people with packs on their backs move away. We also see them go with little carts fully packed with suitcases and boxes. Old and young, mothers and little children. The men are always in uniform except the very old ones. In all our misery we feel rather happy as we sense that the end of the war is coming nearer.

Chapter XVII

The situation with the sick people is not getting better. Dysentery is all around and only the very severe cases are admitted to the Revier. "Revier", it's a fancy word for just a corner of the attic with some straw and a Kiebel. Some have to use it 30 times a day. Some have died already and are for the time being put in the Waschraum. There it is always dark and when it is time to wash yourself you have to find your way around the bodies. It takes four or five days for them to be removed. For just one they won't take the trouble. Once I could recognise a body when it was a bit light. He was like a skeleton and terribly dirty because the floor is always wet and dirty from our shoes. After some time, you become dull to these things and only the loss of a friend matters. We are constantly tired and are always hungry. Even collecting a meal is a tremendous struggle and is always combined with beatings, if not on our backs, then on our heads. One or two of these is enough for several days. A Kapo has beaten Geert S and some others on the head, with a steel ladle which has caused a big hole. The "doctor" has to bandage them up and the ladle has been so badly damaged that it cannot be used anymore. It is believed that the "doctor" is a chemist, a Dutchman who does very little for his countrymen. He may be a prisoner himself, receiving more freedom by saying he is a doctor. He uses toilet paper for bandages — of course it is not very useful, it soils quickly, and falls off. In the Revier is Fre' Lode, my friend.

Chapter XVIII

He has dysentery, but seems to recover. Most of the sick people are Dutchies, and they seem to die more often. According to the doctors, this is due to our constitution. Our lives have been too luxurious, foodwise as well as our ways of living. The hardship of camp life takes too much from us, physically as well as mentally. We are not as hardened as the Russians and the Polish people. They cope much better with a life full of hardship. I see the Dutch boys on their beds wasted to a shadow. You are not able to recognise them anymore. Next to the Kiebel is a young man from Haren, 22 years of age and he is not likely to get any older. He does not even talk anymore. I ask him something but he just stares. He is terribly dirty, as is the person next to him. The straw on which they are lying is soaked and smells unbearable. When others use the Kiebel, it spills over them. It just can't be done any other way. In the evening they die, but they are left there till the next day. Dead and alive mixed together. You get used to it although you do not forget the seriousness of it all. Meanwhile, the SS laugh about it.

The upper attic is not much better, every time there are more cases of dysentery and they can't go to the Revier anymore. The Russians become bolder every day and steal bread out of the room of the Kapos. When it is discovered, they each receive 25 beatings with a stick. After such a punishment, your bottom is black and blue. The Russians pinch anything they can get hold of. One night eight of them escape through a window in the roof and disappear.

Chapter XIX

This means extra roll call, hours on end. All the time counting, reading out names, again counting and so on. Getting up even earlier, hungry and miserable. This in itself makes you sick. On top of that, being so dirty and walking in rags! We have not been able to wash ourselves and the situation becomes unbearable. The next day another group of Russians has escaped. That is it! The commander comes in very early, swearing and raging, pushing and kicking. Roll call! Half-undressed, we run down and stand in the dark, wet laundry. It's the same as yesterday, for hours on end names are called out. Awfully tiring. We are kicked from one end to the other like animals. Again, we go to work without food. Whatever we do get on good days, we eat as quickly as possible to make sure that it will not be stolen. In any case it is never enough to keep any aside. We are getting used to it. At night-time they put Kiebels up in the attic. Only ever to pee, as there is not enough food to do a number two. Downstairs in the Waschraum are 10 Kiebels opposite the pipe with holes. Paper is scarce, but the Russians don't mind at all, they use their fingers. What a situation! At night-time it's awfully hard to find your way to the Kiebel. You need to find your way in the dark over bodies, with much swearing and kicking. You know that you are at the right place when your feet are wet. Finding your way back is not easy either.

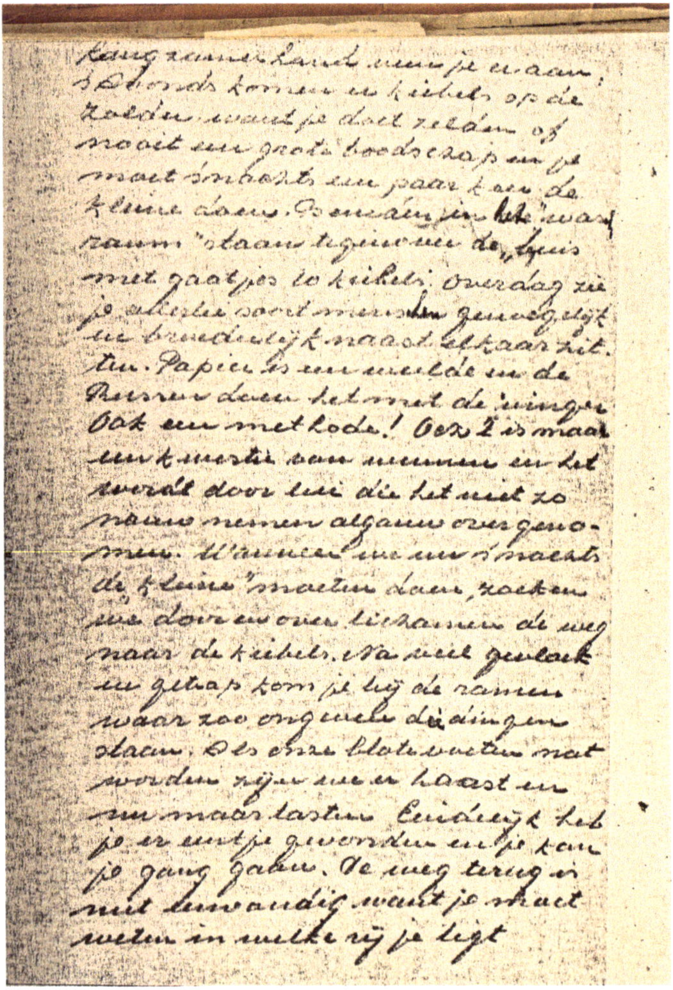

Figure 4: Excerpt from the handwritten memoir of Pieter Laning, Chapter XIX.

Chapter XX

You can't afford to put your shoes on if you have to find the Kiebel in the night. You are sure to be bashed and robbed of them. In the morning one part of the attic is completely soaked. The Russians in particular don't care if they "miss" the Kiebel. The Kapos can't see it anyway, as by now the power station and the water supply are out of order because of damage from the bombing.

Supervision has eased a little and the food has improved somewhat. People are still leaving the city. From a distance we hear the roar of guns and in the night anti-aircraft guns shooting from the railway site. The factory is situated very near to the railway site and consequently the noise robs us of our sleep. But it's going well with the war and that is more important. Still there are many men who can't cope with it all. They go, half dead already, to the Revier. Their last move?

One particular morning, we are again woken up with the hated words "Aufstehen, aufstehen!", a call we have heard a thousand times to wake us up. We receive our regular slice of bread but do not go downstairs for the equally hated "roll call". We don't have to work as the situation regarding the war is very critical. Out of the window, we see large crowds, emptying fully laden freight trains. There are cases with apples and tins full of meat. Everything is handed out. Even the Kapos are getting cases with apples and we each receive two or three of them. I'll never forget the taste of them. They were out of this world! During six months I had not eaten any fruit.

Chapter XXI

We consider it a feast and eat everything in one go. We are getting a few more; this makes us overexcited. Now we long for a cigarette as well, but there aren't any. So we look for dried stinging nettles between the straw and with a little piece of newspaper we make our own. Here anything will do.

The food has to be fetched from the kitchen, which also provides the food for the prisoners of war. Only people from Holland, Belgium or France are allowed to do this job, as some Polish and Russian people have escaped while doing this. Already 25 have escaped. It's considered a privilege to be allowed to go to the kitchen, as you are then able to get a little extra, "organise something", as we call it. You may find a few potatoes or a half-rotten swede. It is all on the scrapheap, occasionally you may find a soupbone, even if it is from a horse, it is a delicacy. Potatoes and the good part of the swede are nicely shared, raw as they are. You just eat anything.

During the night we find ourselves between the English army and the Germans: gunfire from both sides. Shells fall everywhere around our building, night and day there is terrible noise. Planes roar through the sky and shells make a whistling noise all around us. If it were not for the sake of our freedom, we would not be so happy. In the morning the commander tells us that we have to keep quiet and that the city may be handed over without fighting. The English army is getting closer and may be here by three o'clock.

Chapter XXII

Cheers go up and we embrace one another. We cry and shake hands with everyone. We are just crazy. Apart from two, all Kapos have fled out of fear of reprisals from the prisoners as they have caused the death of many. They have often beaten or kicked prisoners to death. In Husem, for instance, 1,500 people died from a transport action of 2,000. They were kicked around and beaten by SS and Kapo. The people there worked from early morning till late at night standing knee-high in water. Ten at a time were kicked into the anti-tank ditches and drowned while their friends watched them. Five hundred returned and 400 of them were just *mussulmen* (walking skeletons) ready for the crematorium.

But that belongs to the past and the commander looks worried when he brings the news to us. We are excited and want to get out, but the guard is still there and whoever wants to get out will be shot. In the afternoon we receive real meat meant for the *Wehrmacht* (the army), but it can't be transported as the railways are badly damaged and the English army is all around. Good for us! We get bread as well and enjoy a few hours of freedom. We don't know if the SS still have some plans for us, but they have packed everything and we hope they will soon go. It looks like it. We thank God for the unexpected freedom and feel so relieved. We don't think anymore of hunger, lice or tiredness. Everything looks bright to us. Planes still fly over and drop bombs, and shells still fall around the factory. We see German tanks go past. We think we will be free very soon.

Chapter XXIII

The day passes by in anxious anticipation and we become more and more worried. The English army has not arrived. Maybe tonight or tomorrow morning? We try to go to sleep but it does not work. We are too tense. We hear the noise of the artillery and the deafening racket of the collapsing of houses that are hit. We wait till the morning and at least have a breakfast of meat and bread. Since the Kapos have left, the Russians have become bolder and force their way into part of the factory where there are suitcases with clothing and other items. They also break into the house of the manager of the factory and take whatever they can get hold of. They come back with trousers, coats, shoes, spoons and forks, all sorts of things, even buckets full of sugar and oats. Up in the attic they start exchanging the goods. Soon the commander arrives and starts using his gun. We go in all directions. Thankfully nobody is hurt. But we hear a new "roll call" and are kicked downstairs by the SS. We have to stand in rows of five and, before we realise it, we are marching towards the freight train and are pushed into the carriages. Totally disillusioned, we look at one another and are wondering what will happen next. After a few hours we are allowed to come out and learn that it was meant as punishment for the stealing and vandalism in the factory. We are quite pleased, as we thought we were being transported or that they would put the machine guns on us when the English army would arrive. We still have to wait patiently but are sure they will come!

Chapter XXIV

But this day also passes by without bringing us freedom. The freight train is still there, but without an engine and the rails are out of order. In the attic the Russians still go on with their trading in secret; however, what food there is is being shared including sugar, jam and apples. It is more than we can cope with, but we can't resist. The result, however, is not so good! We have so much that nearly everyone has diarrhoea. Our liberators have still not arrived and then we hear a rumour that we will be on transport. The commander is nervous, comes up to the attic and when he sees a Dutch fellow trying to open a door, he shoots three bullets through his head. It's a very tense situation — shouts of "roll call" and minutes later we are all in the carriages again. While on our way there, I thought of a chance to escape but it was just too risky with so many guns around. I don't want to risk it, nor do I want the Germans to have the satisfaction of killing me. We are so dismayed and just too flabbergasted to think. Some are crying, others praying and the rest are swearing. It is horrible. We are told the English army was within two kilometres of the city and then turned to the right, leaving the town for what it was. We hear the noise of an engine and minutes later we are going. The sick people are with us, too, but the food and all other things are left behind in the factory. In fear we await what will happen. We are 80 men, in one carriage. It is awfully muggy and we are all in low spirits.

Chapter XXV

Now the misery really starts. Oh, if we had known what would follow! It is the worst time of all. We have many sick people in the carriage. They are already wrecks as it is. Where are we going, that is a question we ask over and over again. We try to sit or stand, whatever is possible. The smell is unbearable, as there is no ventilation. Those who are sick are unable to reach the Kiebel. Some are just soaked with blood as well as with urine. Poor men, they are just broken and have no fighting spirit left in them. They don't care anymore what will happen. They just want to die. We go in the direction of Hamburg and may go back to the camp where we first have been. We don't get any food or drink and are just exhausted and depressed. In the night we indeed arrive in the old camp and with a lot of shouting are pushed into the cellar. Those who died stay in the carriage. The crematorium is close by anyway, about 30 metres. When we come into the cellar, it is already crowded with other prisoners who have been brought here from other places. The smell here is also unbearable, and I lose my mates because of the crowd. We just stand one against the other and so try to sleep. In all this time we have not felt so miserable. We have to watch out not to lose the will to live, else we will never get out and then the road to the crematorium is a very short one. We pray for strength and support and we receive it, too, in all this misery.

Chapter XXVI

Standing between Russians, I come through the night, an endless night full of horror. In the morning I discover that my belt is gone as well as my soap. By six o'clock we are pushed outside, though the fresh air is pleasant. Without any food we have to march to the carriage. Again, we are in there with 80 people, including the sick and a stinking drum. The same misery! A full day of waiting, without straw or blankets. Without moving we begin another night. No food or water or fresh air. For two days we have not received anything at all. It is a terrible suffering, all the more for the sick people and we cannot even give them water to drink. We ask an army officer, but he just laughs at us. The SS walk around the carriages with bloodhounds. When these are let loose, they just tear up anything. They are trained to attack escapees. The following night is just beyond description. People pray to be allowed to die, especially the sick ones. They are desperate. It is very depressing. The night and following day also pass without food or drink. Towards the end of the third day, we start moving. The following morning we receive a slice of bread and a bowl of water. In the camp we found some empty tins and we use those to drink from. Dirty or not, it does not matter anymore. The Kiebel is overflowing, just as well that we came to our destination after one night travelling. When we get out of the carriage, we discover that we are at a seaport. It is Lübeck and is situated at the Baltic Sea. We have to go onto a large ship. It's a freight ship, able to carry 5,000 tons. Those that have survived so far drag themselves onto the ship and we come into a large hold. There are thousands of prisoners and all have to fit in.

Chapter XXVII

We come onto the forepart of the ship and go down 30 metres into the lowest hold, down an iron ladder. It is pitch dark here, we have to feel our way. We let ourselves fall down. It is all iron and icy cold. We receive some thin blankets and try to sleep.

In this hold are several hundred prisoners, many Russians and Poles. We lie down all mixed up, but at least we are able to lie down. After a few hours' rest I agree with some friends to try to get to the middle hold. We feel we may never get out of here, from the bottom, in case something happens. Besides, it is pitch dark here. We can only go up or down one by one and there are a few hundred here. At last we manage to get to the middle hold and feel a little bit safer. Though it is just as dark. We try to get still higher. We act as if we are very sick and call for a doctor as that is our only chance of getting to the upper hold. We manage and it is a bit brighter here, but also full of prisoners. We look for a place where we can spend the night. It is all iron and very cold and there is no Kiebel, but we feel more at ease than right down below, and we even discover a bit of blue sky. We are nevertheless exhausted and try to sleep a bit. All we have we keep on and lie down criss-cross. Hundreds of people all close to death. Nevertheless, people fight for a reasonable place. Nobody wants to be in one of the corners as those are the places where the Kiebels ought to be, but they are lacking. It is a terrible mess as people have to use the corners constantly. Some of the men go 30 times a day, suffering from severe diarrhoea. It is indescribable.

Chapter XXVIII

The worst dysentery sufferers just stay in the corner as they lack the strength or even motivation to get up. They may weigh 40 or 45 kgs and are almost dead, just skeletons. They just relieve themselves where they lie, soon lying in a pool of blood and filth. They have no desire to live anymore, they are apathetic. They are there by the dozens and it is still called Revier (sick bay). We have not been able to wash ourselves for weeks and look like pigs. The smell is unbearable. The nights are worst of all. If you have to get up in the dark, you end up fighting with the Russians and the Poles. They are always in groups and try to take from you the little things that you still may possess. After such a fight you have to call for your friend to find your place back. Even in the daytime the fights begin. If you manage to receive your slice of bread, you have to eat it straight away otherwise the Russians grab you and take it from you even if you have hidden it between your clothes. Every morning when the trapdoor is opened a cable is let down.

Chapter XXIX

All mixed up, unrecognisable, there is a heap of corpses in the corner of the hold. They are filthy, having died in their own body filth, and even covered by the urine or faeces of those who didn't make it to the Kiebel in the dark.

The cable is tied around their waists, and Russians, always prepared to do this task, haul the bodies to the upper deck. Sometimes a corpse catches on the rungs of the steel ladder, but the yanking continues till they are free, and you hear the thump of their landing on the deck. Each morning, there are 10 or 12 dead in each hold, and if you consider there are nine holds, it wouldn't take long for 2,000 men to be eliminated.

The sight of this makes you apathetic in the long run. You sit or lie down most of the day except for collecting a slice of bread and half a litre of what is called soup. This usually goes together with shouting and punching by the Russians and the Poles.

We pray and talk a lot with each other and that encourages us. Sometimes you think you won't survive. It's just not humane anymore. The Russians just take anything from those who are in the process of dying. They are then half-naked when they are drawn up the next morning. Even gold teeth are pulled out of their mouths, something that had often been done in the camp by the SS.

Chapter XXX

One is just not able to stop them doing a thing like this. You simply don't have strength left to prevent it. Life here is just waiting for death and it would mean deliverance for many. Some have no more to wear than singlet and trousers. Socks have not been available for a long time. We just wear shoes on bare feet. Most has been stolen by the Russians. Those that are too weak to collect their food simply go without. The Kapos keep for themselves what is left of the soup and usually that is the better part, as at the bottom there may be some potatoes and vegetables and probably a bit of meat.

So the days pass by and the thirst we experience is unbearable. Sometimes we receive seawater, which makes our suffering worse. Some drink it like beer and just die because of it. If we use it, we only rinse our mouth with it. Geertsema, a vet, Bruinsma, a policeman from Friesland and De Vries from Winschoten are suffering terribly with swollen and infected lips. They are our friends, yet we can't help them. A bottle of water is offered to us by some Russians in exchange for bread. We take it to help the worst ones of our group. When they drink it, it proves to be urine. In the meantime, the bread is gone. That is how they are. If they have a chance, they exchange the bread for cigarettes. Medical care is just nil.

Chapter XXXI

Only the worst cases with infections get some attention and are bandaged with toilet paper. We all suffer from cold and are coughing like mad. No wonder under these circumstances. We now sleep only on our backs as our hips are raw. Five long days we have now been on this ship, and we will never forget it. These days remain in our memories as sheer terror.

From the *Athene* we are now pushed with beatings onto the *Cap Arcona*. This is a ship of 15,000 tonnes and has been used as a passenger ship from the Hamburg–America Line (Germany's answer to Britain's *Titanic*). Here everything is clean and after hours of roll call we crowd 10 people into a cabin for four. Four real beds and a washbasin with running water! We make use of it straight away. It is unbelievable, the dirt that was washed away. We also come to the realisation of what the lice have done to our bodies. It is a sheer pleasure to try to get the lice from our clothes. We never can get them all of course and 20 or so did not mean anything to us anymore. We feel really satisfied and give ourselves a few hours' rest on the ready-made beds. A few hours later we get a few more men in and have to share one bed amongst three persons, not easy but so much better than on the *Athene*. Two days we spend on this beautiful ship. We do nothing but clean our clothes and ourselves. The bottom hold of the ship is for the sick. For them it is a repeat of life on the *Athene*.

Chapter XXXII

The difference, however, is that by now there are hundreds of sick people instead of dozens. The passages are also full, often with those who have already died as there is no way to clear the bodies. Geertsema and Bruinsma are also among them. As I said before, we stayed on the ship for two days.

There are thousands of prisoners as other ships also put theirs onto our ship. It looks like an ants nest. The *Athene* and other ships constantly navigate in our vicinity. We cannot make out in what direction we are going. We see from the porthole that we are close to the shore. We realise that the British Army also come close as we often see shells flying over and hear the noise of planes. The comfort and change of the ship improve our morale. We are still weak and can't make it in one go to the toilet nearby. The food ration has not improved either. After the two days we suddenly have a roll call on deck. We sense that this is not too good. We are already nervous as it is and wonder what will happen next. We realise the danger as we sense that the end of the war is near and the SS could be up to just about anything. We shudder when we see them. The ship is about 200 metres long and on the deck are 2,000 prisoners in rows of five waiting for hours on the orders of the SS.

At last, the *Athene* comes alongside our ship and we have to go back to that ship of horrors. We come into the lowest hold with only the Dutch and Belgians. The Russians had managed to get into the upper hold. We fall down disheartened and each one has to think things through for himself.

Chapter XXXIII

I think of all those I love and feel awfully miserable. Will we ever see them again? But we should not allow ourselves to think along those lines as that is a sure road to death. We still have the will to live and we hope for a miracle. We are completely in the hands of the SS. Hundreds of people actually in one man's hand, for if they put a machine gun at the opening of the staircase not a soul will come out alive. We realise that only God can help us and we resign to that. The night is just as horrifying as the earlier ones, half-sitting, half-lying down on the iron hull. It is very noisy in the air and the drone of British machines gets worse. There are a variety of ships on the water, most of them large and having prisoners on board, also submarines and other warships. It does not seem good to us to be in this position, locked up in a ship. We can't sleep and we try to get upstairs to have a look around. The guard looks for safety from the shells as the anti-aircraft guns are constantly at work. Bombs are dropped on land as well as on the water. Large pillars of fire are visible and we hear explosions close to our ship. We can't stay long on top of the ladder and go down again just waiting for what will happen next. During one of the explosions, while just dozing a bit, we are thrown one over the other. Our ship moves up and down like an empty nutshell. The screams and the noises are terrible, and we think this is the end for us.

Op het groote water varen verschei-
dene schepen van allerlei type.
Een aantal groote schepen met al-
lemaal gewehren, dan tal van
onder zeeërs en andere oorlogsbodems.
Het lijkt ons niet gunstig in deze po-
sitie op een schip te zijn opgesloten.
We kunnen niet slapen en sluipen
zoo nu en dan naar boven en tu-
ren over het zwarte water. De
wacht zoekt steeds dekking
voor de granaatscherven,
want het afweergeschut is steeds in
volle werking. Ook worden op het
land zoowel als op het water bom-
men door de Britten afgeworpen.
Groote vuurzuilen zijn er zichtbaar
en we worden steeds opgeschrikt
door ontploffingen die dicht bij
om schipsplaats vinden. Lang
kunnen we echter niet boven blijven
en we gaan weer naar beneden
en worden gelaten om tot af-
stelling in een dommeling worden we door een geweldige ont-
ploffing door elkaar geworpen.
Een geheele schip wordt als een
notendop heen en weer geslingerd.
Het rumoer en gerommel
is verschrikkelijk en iedereen denkt
dat het nu onze beurt is

Figure 5: Excerpt from the handwritten memoir of Pieter Laning, Chapter XXXIII

Chapter XXXIV

Everyone tries to get to the stairs, but nobody seems to manage to get to the top. When the ship comes right again and nothing more happens, we calm down. It is said that their own men have grounded a submarine close to us. We see, however, that there are three ships on fire. They show up as large pillars of fire and it must be terrible for those on board. When daylight comes, we see the sky full of planes, and ships are like furnaces. We come to the conclusion that one of the ships is the *Cap Arcona*, the one we have been on. There would be thousands of prisoners on board that ship, because when we got off the ship others were put on. Also, our sick people were left on there and at the same time many of our friends. The ships, however, are too far away from us to be able to distinguish anything. We see, however, some lifeboats in the vicinity. It is terrible to look at these ships on fire with so many prisoners on board. And then to know that your own friends are amongst them. Now they will surely die and nobody can save them. They have to choose between the flames and the water, between burning or drowning, as the few lifeboats are immediately full. Our ship has moved during the night and we are now situated near the pier. Planes fly low over our ship and we look for shelter as we are now standing on the deck. The crew is nowhere to be seen. Neither do we see any SS officers and we are thankful for the fact that we are by ourselves close to the pier. Now we can look for ourselves where it is the safest. There are only a few on deck, the majority are still in the hold. Suddenly there is an explosion and our ship is thrown into the air. Everything goes so quickly and we only recover when the first injured people come on deck.

Chapter XXXV

There is terrible confusion. Crying and screaming mingled with the noise of aeroplanes fills the sky. Everyone clambers up the stairs in deadly fear to get out of the lower decks.

Our ship has been hit in the middle and on the decks are many wounded and dead. The moaning and crying are horrendous. Any moment the ship can be hit again, and we try to get to the gangway to get onto the pier. We are stopped by SS soldiers and sent back with gun barrels pointing at us. Wounded people crawl over the upper deck, which is now coloured red with blood. We make our way to the front of the ship, which is high above the pier. Suddenly I have an idea of how to get off the ship as death is surrounding us. I climb onto the rail and get hold of the mooring rope and let myself glide along it until I see the pier underneath me and let myself fall down onto it. How good to be on solid ground and off the ship. Fre' Lode follows me and we start running as fast as we are able to. We fly past a sentry, who fails to see us, as he is busy with many other prisoners. We keep running across the pier and arrive at the harbour. Here it is terribly busy. Thousands of prisoners and all in their striped clothes. Men, women and children. We see dead people on the side of the wharf. Some lie in the water, many are wounded and are without any help.

Between them, screaming SS officers and Grune Polizei. We use this opportunity to get away to the city. Maybe we have a chance to escape because of the confusion. Suddenly we meet up with Gerard Boekhoven, who is from the group "De Groot", and who was arrested on 29 January 1945 together with his wife. We are overjoyed and hug each other. He had the death sentence with many others and was already severely tortured in Neuengamme. "Tied to the gate, 10 lashes on the bare backside with the dog whip." This was because he tried to get some "goodies" out of a Danish Red Cross parcel that he had to collect from barrack 9. He had to crawl underneath a wire that was surrounding barrack 10 where he was. As he was seen (*ezwisehr*) by two SS officers, he was punished by them in view of all the prisoners.

By now he had taken off his ribbon with the word "Torsperre", which was worn on the left arm and was an indication that he, with another hundred people, was going to be hanged (which had happened to many Dutch people). He also had taken off his red triangle with his prison number — H 77389. He said, "Boys, don't give the Germans the opportunity of you being sent by those crazy Nazis into the next world in these last moments. Hide in the masses and try not to be seen." We entrust to him our plan of escape and he decides to join us. We push ourselves, wet as we are, through the crowd. We are on a crossroad.

Chapter XXXVI

We seem to have arrived at a U-boat shed and here are also many unfortunate and miserable people, some bleeding heavily and others badly burnt. They have come from the *Cap Arcona*, many are half drowned. We look for a little while but ignore the hated order "*Zum Funfen*" (in groups of five). We have to go on if we want to save our lives. We don't feel tired or hungry anymore, we have only one thought: to get out of this hell! We go on though there seems to be no end to the row of "striped" people. Thousands of them, some with nursing babies. All of them dirty and skinny. They have been through the same as we have. We walk straight along and then up a slight hill. Prisoners everywhere. In the distance we see tanks coming. We think we are lost now. No chance to escape. There will be tank battles here. We crawl into a ditch. They come closer very fast. Suddenly there is a great movement among the thousands of people. They call out and shout. We see hats thrown into the air. They look like they are possessed. They dance and jump and hug each other. The tanks are very close and we cannot believe our eyes. We are dumbfounded. When the first tank has passed by, we realise: They are British! We cry and laugh. Polish women ask us, "What is going on?" We shout, "The English!" They kiss us and cry. Everyone cries and shouts. A skeleton dancing in the midst of all the misery. Men and women kneeling down to thank the Lord. The tanks roll on by the tens to the harbour. We look around us and we see the British already disarming the German soldiers and even the SS officers who have not managed to get away.

Chapter XXXVII

We see them standing with hands up. We laugh! Oh, what a sight all those Tommies and those joyful people. Between them the sad faces of German soldiers. Oh God, we thank you for this moment of liberation! At long last, "Free." Set free from the grip of those SS devils. There they stand with their hands up, surrendering. Gone is their pride. Now they look pale and worried. The Russians are always in the frontline. They take away weapons from the Germans but also watches and whatever else they can get hold of. We leave it to the Tommies and go our way. We have to take care that we get something to eat. We have not had a thing for at least three days. On a corner of a square stands a large English tank. We go and shake hands with our liberators. We do it with tears in our eyes and are really moved. The Tommies also look at us, then they grab a large box with cigarettes (Players) and give each of us a handful. They also give us chocolate and we tell them what we have gone through. Gerard speaks English quite well, so he tells them of our experience. However, shooting starts again and we say goodbye.

Suddenly an old man stands next to us and speaks to us in Dutch. He is also from Holland and his name is Donker. He tells us that he is a boiler attendant in a large hospital and has his own little room. We can have something to eat with him and probably stay there for the night. We are keen to go with him and look forward to having something to eat and a bed!

Chapter XXXVIII

Also, there will be a comfortable bed, food, cigarettes and sleep, which is just what we need at this time. While walking along Donker tells us that there are still SS officers on the property of the hospital, but that we can reach his room without being seen. It is just on the outskirts of Neustadt. Suddenly we see three officers of the Labour Service, their bikes packed with parcels and ready to leave. They are scared of us and we of them. But Gerard says, "Give us those parcels with food. You have had enough." The last one drops a big loaf of bread and I pick it up. The officer says I may keep it and we go on, pleased with what we got. A little further and we are at the boiler house. We go into Donker's room and fall down on his bed, now realising how tired we are. But first we eat, regardless of the "runs". Bread and butter, bacon and eggs and jam. It tastes fantastic and we eat like horses. We feel as if we are the guests of a king. But suddenly we start to panic. The director of the hospital, who obviously has learned that we were there, comes to Donker and threatens him with a weapon and says we have to leave immediately. But Gerard, who also speaks German quite well, knows his ground. He tells Donker to get an English sergeant with a gun, and off the director goes. Nothing is left of the food. Tomorrow we will see again. Two sleep on one bed and the third one on a mattress on the floor. We have to get up several times because of all we have eaten. Next morning Donker is waiting for us with lots of good things. We enjoy it but have lots of trouble from the lice. Therefore, we burn our hated underwear — together with the hated lice! A great bonfire in the hospital boiler.

Chapter XXXIX

Donker, who has already been out early and heard the latest news, tells us that there is chaos in the city. The Russians have plundered shops and storehouses during the night. They also entered houses and made use of the beds to sleep in. We decide to have a look ourselves. Because of the changed circumstances we feel stronger and dare to take the walk to the city. On our way we meet up with Tommies standing near their tanks and motor vehicles. They offer us cigarettes, biscuits, canned meat and other goodies, which we gladly accept. They can see straight away what kind of people we are, because of our bald heads and the torn and dirty camp clothes. Fine men, each one of them. No shouting or yelling, but calm and polite. They look well and are in good spirits. Fantastic moments for us. It makes us forget that we are tired. They can't tell us anything about Groningen, our home. They had been in Eindhoven and Tilburg in the south of Holland. After spending some time with them, we move on to the city. There it is very busy. German citizens are clearing the streets of barricades under the supervision of British soldiers. Prisoners of war are transported through the city. We loved seeing that! We surprise ourselves that we are able to continue walking without feeling tired. We see people walking with bottles of wine.

Chapter XL

We would like to have some too. We see a warehouse where prisoners are filling bottles out of large barrels. We soon find some bottles too. We fill them up and put them into a bag. I also see chooks and catch one. I wring its neck and put it in the bag with the bottles.

Near the harbour is a U-boat shed and it is filled with canned fruit. A Tommy gives us a hand and soon we are outside with about 40 tins. We find a little cart and put everything on it. In the harbour is a ship belonging to a Belgian. He knows Donker so we leave most of it with him and take only some of it to our room. On board we first eat and drink some and then realise how tired we are. Sitting down doesn't help that, it only makes it worse. At long last we leave and have to rest many times on our way back. We finally arrive at our room, we still have to do a few things such as making the chook ready for cooking. Fre' and I do it together. When it is finished, we lie down but can't sleep, of course. Donker feels obliged to consult a doctor, as we are so close to the hospital anyway.

Chapter XLI

The doctor comes in the evening and gives us a good check-up. The diagnosis is, "Completely weakened through a lack of food." We scarcely weigh 50 kg. He asks us about what we have been eating in the past, though he knows quite well what people suffered in the camps. He has already heard several stories today. The most serious cases have already been admitted and medical staff are busy caring for these cases. We will most likely be admitted to the *Landeskrankenhaus* (hospital). Now we first try and sleep, but I have the runs worse than before. Next to my mattress is a bucket. The intestines of the chicken are also in it. I just can't be bothered to throw them out. Gerard has the same trouble and we take turns. Late in the night, Donker comes to have a look at how we are. I point to the bucket and he takes it to empty it in the toilet. When he comes back, he looks very concerned and tells us we are very sick because he saw so much blood in the bucket. When I realise that what he had seen was the blood of the chook, I cannot help laughing, regardless of how I feel. Nevertheless, we feel worse by the minute. The next morning the doctor tells us we have been allocated places at the hospital. But first we have to get rid of the lice and our clothes have to be burnt. We are washed and scrubbed thoroughly and soon we are in a hospital bed with sheets! The German nursing staff take good care of us. They do what we ask. Yes, that is how they are, either licking or kicking! Soon a doctor comes to check us. This time it is a Pole, he was also a prisoner and freed by the British Army. We don't have to tell him anything. He knows what's wrong.

Chapter XLII

In the camp he was in, he has seen thousands die all from the same thing, a lack of food, exhaustion and mental strain with the result: *mussulman* – crematorium. We will be heading in the same direction if we don't adhere to the instructions given to us. He tells of the terrible things that happened with the *Cap Arcona*, the ship we were taken off at the last minute then transferred to the *Athene*. That ship was bombed in the bay by a British bomber plane and then caught fire. The RAF thought it was a German navy transport, so bombed it. Thousands of former concentration camp inmates, so close to liberty, were drowned or badly burnt. Official data say 6,600. Only about 200 survived. Many of those who died were people we knew from the Revier. This is terrible news for us. We recollect how we saw the ship burning in the night. God has saved us in a very special way. This tragedy happened a few hours after we were transferred to the *Athene*. Also, several doctors died, one of them was our camp doctor, Dr Vlim, who came from Leiden (Holland) and who really helped us when we arrived in the camp. He was the one who pointed out several dangers and the consequences of these events. He always had news about the war and a chat with him would always cheer us up. Brave and stout-hearted Vlim, we will remember you as a good friend. Now that we are here, and so well cared for, we realise how much we owe to him. We are still wrecks but we will be healthy again. We will go back sooner or later and hopefully see our families and those we love again, in good health. We will always remember them and not only we, but the whole nation will and must remember you all. The sacrifice has been too great to be forgotten, may the suffering you went through be an encouragement for our whole nation to regain the unity, which is so much needed. May God grant that Holland may be strong in the future.

Chapter XLIII

The days that follow go past very quickly. We go for x-rays and they show that Gerard has a spot on one of his lungs. It does not seem to be too bad. The doctor says it will clear up with good food and rest. Fre' and I are cleared but we also need rest and good food. We all feel very weak and the doctor tells us this is a reaction to all that we have gone through. The hospital (*Krankenhaus*) is now overcrowded, beds are everywhere, also in the passages. Many, however, don't make it anymore. Every morning we see bodies being carried away. We are not allowed to get out of bed. After a few days I am allowed to try, but I do not get any further than the door. It is impossible. One day a British colonel visits us. This is the result of a chat we had had with a Tommy who would bring us cigarettes every day. We had told him that we had been arrested because we had worked in the Intelligence Service in Groningen. In a special room, we must tell the colonel all about the work we had done. He makes a report of the information we give him and we say goodbye in a very friendly manner. The treatment we receive in the German hospital is good, but the food is far from it. Swedes nearly every day, in the camp we used to get swede soup (*Steckrüben*!). The smell is awful. I can't eat the bread either and give it to Donker who comes to visit us every day.

After some days the British colonel comes to visit us again and tells us that the information we gave him concerning our work in Groningen is correct and therefore we will be transported to a British hospital. We understand that we cannot go home straight away. We have to gain some weight and strength. After that we will be sent to Holland by plane. We will also be considered British soldiers and therefore receive the same privileges. This news excites us as if we were children. A step closer to going home and better food as well. Now it will go fast! In the afternoon we go to the "Packstore" for clothing, which we receive from a Tommy. Germans, under orders of the British Army, have brought in the clothing. Each German family had to bring a complete set of clothing for one person, shoes included, to help prisoners. The clothing is reasonably good, but it does not always fit. Well, at least we are ready for the transport. The ambulance is waiting for us, and we are carried inside on stretchers. After saying our goodbyes, we are on our way to Lüneburg. I sit up so I can see the beautiful surroundings. But one can see that here also the war has been. Several burnt-out cars are on the side of the road. It gives an indication that the Germans gave up rather soon. After two hours we arrive in Lüneburg. We pass the big gates of the former German barracks used by the proud *Deutsche Wehrmacht*, about 30 buildings around a colossal square. The British requisitioned the complex and part of it is now the 74th British General Hospital. Allied soldiers wounded during the recent fighting were being cared for. We are seen straight away by doctors and nurses. They examine us thoroughly. When this is completed, we are allocated a room with patients of different nationalities. The first few days we are seen by doctors, nurses and military social workers who give us chocolates, soap, cigarettes and everything else we need. One of the sisters is Mary Elliott who migrated to Perth W.A. in 1965 and is still living there.

In that 74th hospital we had especially good care (V.I.P. treatment!) and in mid-June 1945 we flew to Eindhoven in a Dakota, and some days later we arrived in Groningen.

Every day we are thankful to have survived these horrors and remember reverently those who were not so blessed.

Pieter Laning H77417

Glossary

Appell	roll call
aufstehen	stand up
Grune Polizei (Ger.)	Civilian police (Green Police)
Huis van Bewaring (Dut.)	Prison
Kapo	Kapos were prisoners, often Jewish, who were forced to serve as stand-in guards
Kiebel (Ger.)	toilet
kranken	sick
Krankenhaus (Ger.)	hospital
Muzelmannen (Ger.) / *mussulmen* (Dut.)	virtual walking skeletons, living but without hope
Revier	sick bay
S.D.	Sieherheitsdienst, the Nazi Party's intelligence agency
schnell	quickly
SS	Schutzstaffel (Protection Squads), major paramilitary organisation for Adolf Hitler, responsible for genocide
Torsperre	those earmarked for death
Waschraum (Ger.)	bathroom
Wermacht (Ger.)	armed forces of the Reich

Acknowledgements

These memories of our father, Pieter Laning, were handwritten whilst he was recovering from malnutrition in an English-controlled hospital in Germany. The memoir was written within weeks of the war ending from his recollection of events since his capture in late 1944 and put in print by his good friend and co-prisoner, Gerard Boekhoven. It was published many years later, in 1980, just a couple of years before Dad passed away. The memories were too painful to do it earlier.

Soon after the booklet arrived at our home, our mother translated it into English to enable us to read it and the translation was typed up by our sister-in-law Hetty Laning. As English was not Mum's native tongue, her translation was edited by Peter van der Schoor to improve English expression, to add some omissions and improve grammar.

I am indebted to Peter for his good work and to Melita Eagling for preparing it for publication.

Klaas Laning
May 2023

The author and the translator

Figure 6: Pieter and Dineke Laning, 1976

Pieter Laning and Dineke Mulder grew up in the Netherlands, living in the same general area of Groningen. During the war they had both been incarcerated and suffered torture due to engagement in resistance activities but did not meet until some time after. Despite earlier opposition from Dineke's father, Pieter and Dineke were married on 1 April 1947 and moved into a second-floor unit in Samarang Straat—an Indonesian district in Groningen—where their three eldest children were born. They lived there until October 1950 when they departed by boat for Tasmania. It was much later that Dineke decided to translate Pieter's memoir, ensuring it was accessible to their now much larger family.

www.ingramcontent.com/pod-product-compliance
Lightning Source LLC
Chambersburg PA
CBHW040243010526
44107CB00065B/2861